smart storage

smart
storage

**Stylish solutions for
every room in your home**

Joanna Copestick & Meryl Lloyd

photography by **Andrew Wood**

RYLAND
PETERS
& SMALL

For Brian and John, thank you for

remaining sane while all around was chaos

First published in Great Britain in 1998
by Ryland Peters & Small
Cavendish House
51–55 Mortimer Street
London W1N 7TD

Text copyright © 1998
Joanna Copestick and Meryl Lloyd
Design and photographs copyright
© 1998 Ryland Peters & Small

A CIP catalogue record for this book is available
from the British Library.

ISBN: 1 900518 66 X

Printed and bound in China by Toppan Printing Co.

Designer Ashley Western
Editor Zia Mattocks
Location Researcher Nadine Bazar
Location Research Assistant Kate Brunt
Stylist Melanie Molesworth
Project Consultant Karina Garrick
Production Manager Meryl Silbert
Creative Director Jacqui Small
Publishing Director Anne Ryland

Jacket credits
Front: Ian Bartlett & Christine Walsh's house in London;
back left: David Jermyn's house in London designed by Woolf Architects;
back above right: a house in London designed by François Gilles &
Dominique Lubar, IPL Interiors.

Contents

Introduction

There was a time when it was exceedingly difficult to get excited about storage, but all that has changed as space becomes more precious and belongings and technology accumulate at an alarming rate. Storage has become one of the most flexible and inventive factors of home planning. Sorting out furniture and belongings and keeping them ordered and accessible has become a spiritual quest for the contemporary home owner. Where once was dull necessity, there is now a creative pursuit, a challenge that has to be met and needs that have to be resolved.

Storage is often a good starting point for designing a home from scratch. Thinking about your possessions, present and anticipated, is a good way of working out what your real needs are in terms of space, light and furniture in your living space. In order to make your storage solutions work, you have to take a careful look at the kind of person you are. Someone who throws everything on the nearest available surface could benefit from a disciplined structure, where a labelled place for everything would motivate a lackadaisical approach. A more ordered personality probably already has a sense of where things go and would allocate objects to natural homes close to their place of use.

As we accumulate more and more possessions, technology and information, there is an increasing need for simpler homes that provide a calm space conducive to relaxation, in which to unwind and escape the telephone, fax and door bell. Organized living has become paramount as a way of controlling the work pressures, time demands and fast pace of life that better communications and travel have brought to our everyday existence. Why sort through a pile of newspapers and children's drawings only to find a stack of unpaid bills and flyers for films and plays that have already been and gone? Good storage will ease the pressure and calm the mayhem: life is too short for chaos.

A way of life

Contemporary living makes so many demands on time, money and space that, with our ever-increasing need to gather possessions around us, storage has become a buzz word for home owners. Good storage is held up as one way in which the quality of life can be improved, enabling you to create time for more rewarding pursuits.

Sorting out your storage needs and planning your living space accordingly is all a matter of working out a balanced view of how you live, how you want to live, and how you think you will be able to live. While a gloriously minimal kitchen with nothing on display may appeal to the control freak within, it is no use trying to impose an impossible order on a life that thrives on chaos. Yet if you feel as though you are constantly searching for mislaid items, such as scissors or keys, perhaps it is time to examine ways to simplify your life.

The obvious starting point is to define how you live, then you can prioritize your storage needs according to your lifestyle. If you are a keen gardener, for instance, you will inevitably have numerous books and plenty of tools and paraphernalia, and if you have children, there will be ever-growing collections of toys, furniture and leisure kit to contend with. Once you have carefully analysed what you need to store, think about where best to store it. Will you need instant access to everything or can some items be tidied away in inaccessible cupboards or out of the house altogether? Making your space work for you – every single corner of it – will enable you to relax in the area that is left.

Take a critical look at your existing storage space and decide whether it is adequate or whether you will need to make structural alterations or buy additional pieces of furniture to fit everything in. Perhaps you could knock two rooms into one to make a larger space, and then devote a whole wall to built-in or freestanding

Top right **A container shaped like a giant hat box hides unsightly clutter and doubles as a bedside table.**

Centre right **Glass-lipped drawers are sleek, clean and user-friendly, as their contents are always readily discernible.**

Bottom right **Distressed almost to distraction, this cupboard has seen life. Pitted, worn surfaces are often more interesting than refined, clean-lined pieces that dare not hide real clutter.**

Bottom left **Filing cabinets become storage drawers for hats, gloves and shoes in an industrial-style cloakroom tucked behind sliding frosted-glass doors.**

Opposite top left **Purpose-built shelves define a corner and enable toys and books to be stored on display in an accessible manner.**

Opposite centre left **An Indian trunk shows that storage need not be obvious. Intricate carving and distressed paint effects render this box decorative as well as practical.**

Opposite bottom left **White shoe boxes tuck neatly into purpose-built slots that are generous enough to display shoes and their containers.**

Opposite far right **Baskets are versatile containers for everything from home-office clutter to toys and magazines.**

This page **Serene order** follows the strong, regular lines of this home office where even the hi-fi and television slip unobtrusively between neat wall units of drawers and shelving.

Right top **Kitchens are sometimes best treated as angular planes of activity, the finished result being scrupulous order and calm.**

Right centre **A bold-coloured, geometric mini dresser with a versatile combination of cupboards, shelves and drawers prove that storage can be fun.**

Right bottom **Use unexpected containers, such as this battered case, to hold the unattractive necessities of modern living – audio tapes and CDs, or your worst bills.**

Far right **A giant-sized mirror salvaged from former glory makes a perfect centrepiece in a big, white hallway.**

units? Choosing between single pieces of furniture and built-in options depends a lot on the available space, but as a general rule, built-in cupboards and shelves take up less space and work more efficiently than stand-alone items, especially in kitchens.

Editing the contents of each room in an ordered manner – however disorganized you are by nature – is a necessary chore to start the process. The task will seem less daunting if you set a time limit and confine your efforts to one drawer, one cupboard or one room at a time. Often a determination to clear a lot of clutter at once is thwarted as you find yourself dwelling on old diaries, photographs and gifts from jilted lovers. Sort your possessions into piles, containing the emotion for as long as it takes to create the most satisfying pile of all, marked 'out'. Out of the cupboard and out of your life, to yield more space for everything else.

Left **Display collections in a way that enhances and emphasizes their finer points. Period shoes are perfectly aligned in almost comical regimentation.**

Bottom **See-through containers do not have to be scrupulously organized.**

Opposite top left **Shelves and cupboards recessed around a door are perhaps the most space-saving solution for any room.**

Opposite bottom left **Battered cupboards with many compartments mean that hoarders can hide their furtive collections of shells, stamps or audio tapes.**

Far right **There will never be arguments in a bathroom with two sinks on generous cupboards and a long mirror.**

Categorize discarded clothes, china, unused presents or worn-out furniture according to whether they should go to the charity shop, recycling centre or simply into the bin. Garage or car-boot sales are a good way of off-loading unwanted objects – you can always go home via the dump to rid yourself of what's left over.

Create another pile for everything you need to keep but don't want cluttering up the bottom of the wardrobe or lurking in a drawer: photographs, letters, newspaper cuttings, seasonal clothes and decorations, and such like. Buy boxes, baskets or files and label everything that goes into a loft, shed, garage or cupboard. Store everything you decide to keep with other similar items: mixing up too many disparate objects is a sure way of losing them.

What you are left with should be only the necessary and the beautiful: those items that you need to store close to hand for frequent use and objects that demand to go on display, whether on walls or shelves, or as freestanding pieces.

Creating space

Making alterations to the structural elements of your home can often yield unexpected and fantastic results. Tearing out a false ceiling, for example, or making one really tall, airy room instead of two low ones will give dramatic impact to the space, as well as creating extra height and much more wall space for hanging, displaying and building into. Knocking through two smaller rooms to create one large space often produces more light, and tucking cupboards, rooms and windows into the eaves will give you space you never knew existed before. It is all a matter of opening your mind to the less obvious solutions that your home presents, looking at a space with a sense of vision from all possible angles, and searching out ever-more ingenious ways to use whole rooms, rather than just a part of them, as effectively as possible.

While many architectural storage solutions are born of a fascination with minimalism – a sense of order and calm often go hand in hand with a compulsion to contain belongings in strict regiments of flush-fitting cupboards – it doesn't have to be a lifestyle choice. One wall in a bedroom or living room fitted with sleek floor-to-ceiling cupboards may be all you need to hide a serious music collection, a library of children's videos and five-years' worth of your favourite magazines. There is something undeniably appealing about a neat wall that gives the appearance of control and space while concealing a tawdry conglomeration of old batteries, broken toys and spare plugs. For those who yearn for a pristine white space with no visible objects on display, fitting some simple streamlined cupboards may be all that is required to help you achieve this. The thought of preserving the symmetry created by the clean lines may be enough to persuade you not to give in to a natural inclination to leave correspondence, books and newspapers lying around – you may even find yourself inspired to keep their contents in order, too.

Opposite **Floor-to-ceiling control is what you need to achieve a successful approach to minimal living. The taller the cupboard, the more junk you can cram in.**

Left **In a cool, calm white space the recessed kitchen worktop is deliberately painted black so that, come evening, dirty plates can be piled up and not even seen among the subtle overhead lighting.**

Below **An unobtrusive under-counter unit opens to reveal order within. A row of inviting glasses in a clean, sparse cupboard is some-thing to be proud of – a sense of order that is reflected in the out-ward appearance of this kitchen.**

19

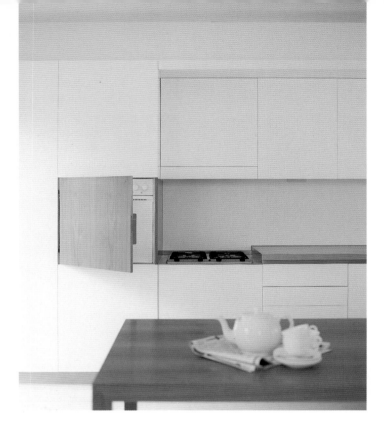

It is obviously easier to incorporate architectural solutions during the early stages of planning or redesigning a space, but individual rooms can be altered one at a time, too. Refitting a kitchen may give you a chance to break away from using more traditional materials and layouts and go for a bolder approach, while knocking two rooms into one gives you a chance to treat the whole of one side of the room in a different way, using low-level cupboard units, integral shelving or raised flooring with storage beneath. The materials you choose are important if you wish to match the storage with existing architectural features or fittings.

Adding on rooms in the form of loft conversions, basements, garages, sheds and conservatories will provide additional living and storage areas. In small spaces, sliding doors, pull-down beds, cupboards that contain televisions or pull-out ironing boards, and cupboards with concertina doors concealing storage systems on castors, are all good ways of making use of space. Take inspiration from the compact living spaces in barges and motor homes.

Left **When even the oven is tucked away behind a door, you know there is a serious minimalist at work. The message is clear – nothing but ultimate tidiness will do in this kitchen.**

This page **Plain cabinets embrace the different elements of a kitchen, a home entertainment area and an extensive book and piano-music collection, without anyone having a clue as to the contents of the room.**

Rooms for storage

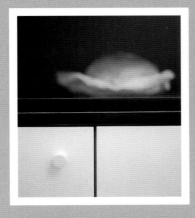

An ordered environment has an undeniably calming effect, and if you are the kind of person who never manages to file the bills, find the spare buttons or locate a new bulb, take a fresh look at your home room by room. We have divided the home into fluid, individual zones, where activities, relaxation and access to your belongings is treated as a series of life cycles, instead of examining storage solutions in isolation – a holisitic approach. Think about the natural path belongings follow around the home and identify the best place to store them. Many items, such as clothes, follow a circular track from wardrobe to laundry basket to the wash, requiring several storage solutions en route. Creating an easy path through these stages is as vital as allocating unobtrusive storage that merges into the surroundings with ease, making everything accessible and usable.

A place where

the living is easy

the pleasure centre

Living rooms are different things to different people. In some homes a living space is the one room in the house in which the whole family congregates to relax, entertain and play. In others, it is a more formal space into which guests are invited, and the television is banished to another room. Sometimes a living room doubles up as a work space, an eating area or a playroom. Work out your priorities and what you use the room for most, then plan your storage accordingly, so it works best for you.

A room in which you read, relax and entertain guests is one space where large, freestanding cupboards make a lot of sense. Often characterful old pieces, such as a battered dresser, an antique armoire or even an old metal school cupboard are perfect for concealing video tapes, audio cassettes, home entertainment centres and the 'to file' pile. Many people prefer to store at least part of their book collection in the living room, since it is the place where you are most likely to find some spare time to start or finish reading a novel. If there are no convenient alcoves in which to fit shelving or cupboards, devote part or all of one wall to a line of deep, invisibly mounted shelving.

Pass a critical eye over your existing storage and furniture arrangements. The advantage of

having a house full of unfitted furniture means you are able to move pieces around as demands and tastes change. Glass-fronted cabinets, pigeon-hole shelving units, open shelves and linen cupboards will all work equally well whether they are in a kitchen, a bedroom, a study or a living room, giving you the freedom to move pieces from room to room as your needs alter. Modular systems are a convenient halfway house between freestanding units and built-in solutions. Take your pick from a huge variety of decorative styles and configurations to enable you to achieve exactly the right combination for your specific needs.

In the same way that kitchens can be revamped by changing or painting the cupboard doors and replacing the door furniture, so alcove cupboards in the living room of a recently purchased home can be similarly altered to suit your taste. In time, you may be able to have a carpenter refit the space with your own design. If you do, start by finding pictures of similar systems in a magazine or book, make a rough sketch and discuss your ideas with a joiner. If you are not planning to stay in your home for more than a couple of years, it is probably not worth considering building in too many cupboards and wardrobes. Although ample storage is often a good selling point, the chances are the new owners will want to impose their own decorative style on existing cupboards and shelving systems.

The most expensive items in a living room are usually the seating arrangements. If space is short, you may prefer to have a sofa bed instead of a large armchair, or an ottoman that will double up as a side table or coffee table. Choose pieces of furniture that have

Whether your preference is for built-in or freestanding options, choose pieces of furniture with multipurpose uses.

Home entertainment can become an unmanageable, unsightly clutter without proper shelves, cupboards or racks.

multipurpose uses. Low-level coffee tables that incorporate drawers will easily hide books, magazines and candles, while nests of tables – a great space saver – are no longer considered passé. Gate-leg tables can transmute from small display areas when they are folded up, to miniature desks for homework or bill-paying when extended.

Make sure your storage exists happily alongside the decoration and architectural style of your space without compromising the visual impact of the room or its relaxing function. Exploit the existing architecture, whether it is alcoves on either side of a fireplace, a tall,

fitted corner cupboard or a square-bayed window that lends itself to a window seat with under-bench storage. Picture-rail shelves and Shaker-style peg rails make good display areas at a safe distance above rampaging children, while on the floor old trunks, blanket boxes and lidded baskets are good movable options. Slim alcoves between large casement windows can be fitted with narrow

shelves and cupboards, while wide doorways can be enhanced with book shelves that fit around and above the door frame.

Don't forget the quirky solutions; they are often the best. Make use of redundant industrial furniture, such as utilitarian filing cabinets fitted with castors, battered old school lockers and catering-style metal shelving. Old baker's trolleys make smart movable homes for ever-increasing piles of current magazines, books or videos, while disused plan chests are perfect for preserving a precious collection of children's artwork and paperwork.

Display is important in a living room, since it is the place where you are most likely to want to view and admire favourite collections and treasured objects. Good lighting is just as important for highlighting groups of pictures in a graphic arrangement as it is for spotlighting small objects in a wall-mounted glass display case. Uplighters will enhance any treasure placed along a picture rail, while a simple halogen table lamp will throw a pool of light onto favourite picture frames, glass vases or ornaments.

Organically shaped frameworks will often elevate a repetitive collection of objects, such as old tin toys, football cards or ornaments, to a well-considered piece of display. An array of similar-size

Create a stress-free living space which is conducive to relaxation.

pieces arranged and displayed together in a sensitive manner will make a pleasing, personal addition to any living space.

Baskets make attractive, versatile and useful storage options. Brightly coloured flat-bottom varieties with handles can be used to transport magazines and other reading matter around the room. Log baskets beside the fireplace are decorative and functional. Large box-shaped versions will house newspapers and books, while smaller ones are perfect for spare change, keys and recent receipts. Small-scale storage is a good way of combining clutter-control with display: miniature chests of drawers, wooden boxes and Shaker swallowtail oval boxes are all visually appealing yet practical.

Cool, calm and under control

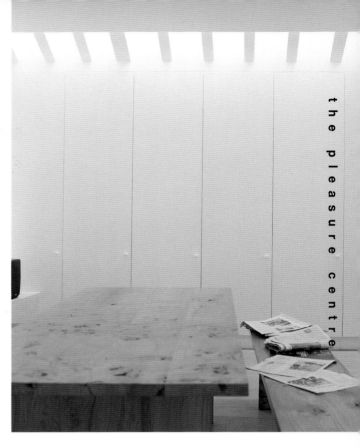

Left **Serenity is the only possible state of mind in a carefully considered living space where everyday junk has retreated behind sleek, regular cupboard doors.**

Above top **Large shallow drawers hold a serious tape collection, so each is visible.**

Above **Hiding the hi-fi may not be everyone's ideal, but it helps maintain the clean lines of a pristine space.**

Above right **There may be chaos concealed behind these measured doors.**

When a space is planned from the start with integral storage in mind, the architecture of the room merges easily with its contents, as each piece of furniture can be selected to work with the others to complement the natural contours of the room. Here, clean white lines and a rich mix of textures and materials combine to create visual peace in a converted mews house. The contemporary-style floor-to-ceiling cupboards and discreet benches that open to allow for more storage mean that everyday clutter is effortlessly hidden from view, allowing the soft lighting and a sense of control and restraint to come to the fore. The honest, hard-working qualities of the natural materials used – wood, stone and leather – create a surface harmony that does away with a need for pattern or paraphernalia.

Words and pictures

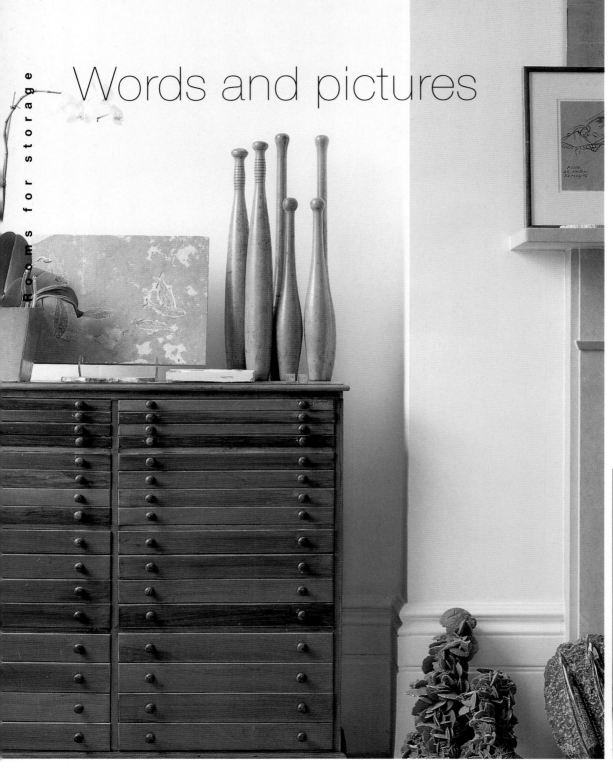

Placing works of art and books so they are easy to access yet pleasing to the eye is often a problem in living areas that demand to be relaxing retreats. A large collection of books can be visually disturbing and too dominant, but placing them in glass-fronted cabinets or behind sliding panels or swivel cupboard fronts helps contain their presence, while the dead space of cupboard doors may be used to display pictures. Filling cupboards below book shelves leaves the rest of the room free for furniture.

Opposite far left **A striking cherry wood ethnological display cabinet is also home to carved wooden clubs and ancient fossils.**

Opposite left **Perspex™ cubes double as side table and display cabinet without seeming to take up any space.**

Left, above and below **A picture gallery is simply a cupboard door, which opens to reveal books and more pictures.**

This page **Cantilevered cupboard doors slide along curved grooves to serve as window shutters, mock walls and display space – truly multifunctional.**

Open house

A functional approach to storing the things you need around you is a good way of turning necessities into decoration. In an industrial-inspired living area, open book shelves abut glass-fronted cupboards that are actually a kitchen larder. Every space on the two walls has been used, leaving the floor clear for basic, well-considered furniture – like the long table that serves as both a work station and dining area. The shelves are on adjustable brackets to accommodate all shapes and sizes of books, boxes and files, while under part of the bottom shelf are shallow drawers for tapes and stationery. The glass panels along the other wall create colourful reflections from the wall of books and the plants on the decking outside. Within the cupboards are china, glasses, food and appliances, which are handily close to the kitchen area on the right, and to the table. The antithesis of a minimal aesthetic, yet contemporary in its approach, this is a modern Aladdin's cave.

Above **Open-plan living spaces demand that storage is practical and placed exactly in the area where it is needed. Here, the four walls of one huge room each have their own particular function.**

Right **Library meets office on a wall devoted to books and files. There is no excuse for not finding a particular file, book or photograph within such a visible and comprehensive display of the written word.**

Sound and vision

Opposite **Placing the television on open shelving among a large magazine collection integrates it very well and prevents it from becoming a dominant feature in the room.**

Left **Packing a hi-fi cabinet into an appealing slatted cupboard is one way of de-teching the living room.**

Above **Small CD boxes stacked on industrial metal shelving make their own storage system.**

Above right **A hi-fi tucks neatly into a shelf space under a run of wall cupboards and is at a perfect height for easy use.**

Music, television and radio are indispensable in a living space where you can kick off your shoes, forget the outside world and learn to relax. The disguise-versus-display debate often rages here. Many music buffs would never dream of hiding cherished albums, CDs or tapes in cupboards or boxes, whereas others might yearn to hear but never see them. Either way, the answer is to store the hi-fi close to the music collection, in the area where you most listen to music. Drawers in units or on castors, shelves, alcove cupboards and free-standing units are all possible solutions, but cabinets should allow the air to circulate, as hi-fi units emit heat and need to breathe. Hi-fis sound better kept off the ground, as do speakers unless they are on integral stands. Integrated storage systems that house all the technology, including the hi-fi, television, cable and satellite decoders, and even a computer are available in many designs for every architectural period.

Balance, scale and perspective

Opposite **Floor-to-ceiling cupboards and a concrete fireplace merge organically with the architectural knocked-through space.**

This page **Narrow geometric cupboards with sharp-angled handles extend all the way up to the roof to shield all manner of unwanted mess from view.**

Architect-designed homes often display a great respect for storage and what it can do to a space. Designing storage so it enhances a room, extends the architectural story and fulfils the functional needs is a strong consideration in homes where specific belongings and attitudes push the design in a certain direction. Here, a collection of books and magazines had to be incorporated in a clean, pared-down space, where the supreme quality of every piece of furniture, fitting and fixture dictates the pace. In a neat recess, chunky, invisibly supported shelves are lent importance but don't dominate. Above a stone fireplace surround is a thick-lipped mirror of the same width, and in the centre of the room a square table reflects the sharp angles of the slatted seats. All is symmetrical, balanced and calm.

Above **A gnarled ladder lies along a shelf in a quirky acknowledgement of the sharp lines and right angles.**

Right **Smooth surfaces and strict lines are softened by a rug and banquette-style sofa.**

Boxed away and stacked up high

Above, left to right **Wooden oval boxes make an elegant display that doubles as a drinks cabinet; a versatile freestanding unit can be used for a variety of functions – side or bedside table, vegetable store or toy chest; a casual stack of colourful boxes makes an attractive display.**

Opposite right **Order is imposed by a collection of boxes that slot neatly into made-to-measure shelves.**

In any living space, there will always be myriad small items that regularly need tidying up and containing, often at the end of a busy day or after a weekend of entertaining when you most need to surround yourself with order and establish a sense of calm. Freestanding furniture, baskets, boxes and trunks in interesting shapes and a variety of sizes can hide everything from magazines and holiday brochures to photograph albums and oversized books.

Whatever you need to store, unexpected, unusual units with a hint of humour will disguise all sorts of uninspiring, unattractive items, as well as livening up the surroundings. For tiny objects, use old decorated

This page **Different-sized units of the same design are graphic statements of good organization.**

cake tins, large glass or pottery jars, galvanized buckets or deep willow baskets. Concealed drawers, old tin trunks and blanket boxes also look decorative as well as serving a practical function.

Rather than store small boxes on wall-mounted shelves, incorporate them into a display by piling them up high on the floor or stacking them against a sofa for a small, instant side table. Low-level coffee tables with integral drawers can hide a surprising quantity of clutter – even the remote control can claim a home – and provide another surface for display.

Mixing old and new

Opposite **Arched windows throw light on 1960s furniture and modular storage.**

Left **A multifunctional coffee table is an asset in a compact space.**

Below **Matching bowls make decorative containers for small change or keys.**

Part of a large house that has been converted into a compact apartment combines contemporary design with traditional architectural strengths and features. Low-level cupboards tuck underneath lift-up shelves, with a slab of slate in the centre to create a sleek hearth for a recessed fireplace that doffs a cap to 1960s design. On either side, cube-like flush-fitted wall cupboards are interspersed with alcove shelves to form mini storage systems.

A sense of order is preserved with a low-level coffee table that has three pull-out drawers, a large wooden trunk and several wicker baskets for magazines and books. In quite a small space, keeping clutter tucked behind cupboards and on the wall allows the rest of the room to be devoted to necessary furniture.

Opposite left **A makeshift vase in the form of a battered and rusting metal jug is perfectly at home on a rough-hewn mantelpiece.**

Opposite top right **Jugs and other small items, such as cups and saucers, candlesticks and tiny boxes, create small displays interspersed with books on a shelf.**

Opposite below right **A graphic chequerboard of built-in cupboards and shelves calls out for favourite pieces to be displayed among the book collection.**

Right **A delightful glass-fronted linen cupboard makes a versatile, multifunctional piece of furniture in a living space.**

Details on display

Finding the right home for your favourite vase, jug, bowl or plant container, where it is always easy to locate and access when you want it, is sometimes an organic process that evolves depending on how firmly your chosen piece demands to be on display. Another time, you may find yourself with a specific piece of built-in shelving which is crying out for a graphic display of disparate objects or collected treasures and would look empty and unfinished if it were not filled. Or, you may have a glass-fronted cabinet that needs filling with careful attention to detail and aesthetics, rather than simply cramming it with whatever comes to hand. Display that works can truly be an uplifting aspect of storage.

Kitchens that

function with style

energy store

The kitchen is the one room in the home where fundamental storage requirements have to be addressed but limitless solutions are on offer. The idea of the fitted kitchen first developed in the USA during the 1920s, where small larder cupboards evolved into the fitted units we find in kitchens everywhere today. They remain a potent influence on how we plan the hub of the home, complete with catalogues that ache with mind-numbing gadgets for keeping the vacuum-cleaner tubes straight, mugs well hung and spice jars firmly attached to cupboard doors. While some of these are undeniably useful and ingenious, others are just time wasters. The trick is to see past the gimmicks to the cool solutions.

During the 1990s the trend in kitchen design has been to veer away from the strict uniformity and constraint of lines of units ranged around a room. Yet cupboards topped with work surfaces are a system that works well, and in a small kitchen fitted units still make the best use of space. They can be made more flexible by adding trolleys or shelving units on castors underneath the worktop. If finances are tight, this is a good way of preserving some space for when you can stretch to a dishwasher. In the meantime, you can use the space for hiding the recycling bin or unsightly cleaning equipment.

To sort out the kitchen and get to grips with the storage issues, start by looking critically at all your kitchen equipment. Lay it out on the kitchen table, including every last piece of unused wedding-present china, seldom-seen baking tins, sad-looking casserole dishes and discarded electric carving knives. Edit individual pieces with several criteria in mind. When was it last used? Has it past its 'styled-by' date? Is it simple to use or do you always cut your fingers on it? Does it waste time rather than save time? Divide everything into three piles

for a garage sale, the dump and hand-me-downs, and then store any sentimental heirlooms out of the way in the loft or cellar.

Then separate everything you have left into four categories. Think about each item and decide whether you need it readily accessible for everyday use, you must keep it on display because it is pleasing to look at or is always needed, you can happily relegate it to the back of a cupboard for use only twice a year, and, most importantly, you don't know why you've hung on to it for so long. This last pile embraces all the items you think you can't throw away yet. Put these at the back of a cupboard and make a note to check them again in three months' time. If you still haven't used them, they simply have to go.

Don't forget all the paperwork too. Some say that if you keep only one drawer in the kitchen for miscellaneous clutter, then that is as much as you can accumulate. The more nooks and crannies you

Spring cleaning the cupboards on a regular basis helps keep the kitchen functional and under control.

devote to junk mail, spare batteries and stationery, the more chance there is to overfill them with items that never see the light of day.

Once you have filled a few refuse sacks you will probably have edited down the contents of your kitchen to a manageable level. This process is worth doing annually at least, even if you aren't planning to rip out the kitchen and start again. Judicious evaluating, editing and restocking that leaves you with a clean, sorted cupboard full of good things is a satisfying chore that is always appealing. Learn to live with less; it will lighten your load, physically and spiritually.

Once edited, divide your belongings into functional groups. Cooking equipment and appliances in one corner, china and crockery in another, cutlery and table linen in another. You will find that a natural order emerges. If you are planning a kitchen from scratch, decide how you are going to live in it. If there is an eating area as well, you may want to store some table linen and glasses close to that spot. If the space benefits from a high ceiling, a hanging rack could be an ideal space-saver.

Make the most of any architectural features that will make planning kitchen storage an easier task.

An existing fireplace alcove calls out for a cooking range, freestanding dresser or sideboard built to fit. Make sure you cover the range in scale, taking into account everything from your large saucepans and cumbersome food processors to tiny tea strainers, mustard spoons and nutmeg graters. Small storage containers, large built-in or freestanding cupboards, pull-out larders and vegetable racks on castors, baskets to slot under surfaces and wall-mounted racks for utensils are all simple solutions that make a kitchen work efficiently, aesthetically and safely.

Next work out what existing storage there is and what can be added. In a kitchen where, despite getting rid of lots of items, storage space is still tight, look at the walls and see if there is any space left for additional shelving or cupboards. If there is floor space available, buy a butcher's block or trolley on castors for moving food, china or homework from one area to another.

Food shopping is not undertaken as frequently as it once was. We tend to buy in bulk once a week or even less often, so more food needs to be

stored at any one time. Big fridges are one of life's necessities, and all perishable foods should be stored there. There is no sight more pleasing than a generously proportioned fridge, well organized and interestingly filled. For maximum life, fresh vegetables should be kept in a dark place where the air can circulate freely. Try to keep all your cooking necessities, such as olive oil, oriental sauces, condiments and spices, close to the stove, and have pulses, pastas and noodles, displayed or in a cupboard, close to hand, so you don't have to keep walking from one area of the room to another while you're cooking.

Display is a strong element of storage in kitchens. Making a virtue of appliances, utensils and equipment means throwing out chipped and ugly china and saucepans and replacing them, over time, with your favourite materials and makes. Stainless-steel and copper pans, pleasing toasters, coffee makers and a gleaming muti-purpose food processor are beautiful objects in their own right. There is no need to hide them away behind cupboard doors if they are in constant use. China is another element that makes a great display while being easy to access. Display everyday pieces close to the dishwasher to make the lifecycle work for you, not against you.

Keep stylishly designed appliances and small-scale storage solutions on display, freeing up cupboards for other items.

Fresh fruit, bottles of mineral water and ample supplies of wine can be good to look at as well as useful, along with vases, big bowls and baskets. The following pages show the sheer scope of workable, imaginative solutions for the energy store.

From store to store

Storing food is, in a sense, a matter of re-cycling. The process begins the moment you bring food home from the shop. Individual items are categorized and put away, only soon to be removed, prepared, cooked, eaten and the waste discarded in a cycle as constant as life itself.

This page **A range of flush-fitted units slotted neatly beneath chunky marble countertops blend subtly with the white walls, providing a neutral backdrop for the kitchen table, where the shopping can be dumped, ready for sorting.**

Right above **Keep all of your fresh vegetables in a cool place, out of the light and in a container that allows the air to circulate.**

Right centre **Pasta always looks its best – and is easy to identify – stored in transparent containers.**

Right below **Wine bottles make a graphic display in the right kind of rack.**

Top **A big fridge eases the burden on storage elsewhere in the kitchen.**

Above left **Think laterally and use unexpected storage containers, such as glass** measuring beakers, which look cool filled up with long ribbons of pasta.

Above right **Grade fruits and nuts by shape in glass tanks for simple visual order.**

51

Freestanding

Strong, dominant colours create a powerful impact in this kitchen where chunky, free-standing wooden units create a sense of the built-in. On an industrial metal shelving system against a sharp red backdrop, a visual drama is played out by an eclectic combination of pasta and pulses, cookery books, a microwave, pots and pans.

The freestanding units are all designed in the same style, but each one has a unique function. A cooking zone centres around a central hob with a

units for flexibility

worktop on either side with shelves underneath, perfect for cooking trays and oversized bowls. The washing zone comprises sink, dishwasher and cupboards which, lacquered in a shade of red that sings with vitality, shine above the stone floor. The central island is primarily for food preparation and has large pigeonholes in which everyday china and glasses are stacked ready for use, making the trip from the dishwasher opposite an efficient operation. On one side of the counter are small, square drawers that contain pots of herbs, tea bags and other clutter-inducing objects. The island encourages people to stand and linger against its bar-style countertop.

Left **Generous freestanding units are simple, but ultra-effective, combining open shelving, concealed cupboards, pigeonholes and drawers for versatile and flexible storage.**

Right **An island work station incorporates handy drawers for clutter. A useful, movable spice rack on the counter holds glass vials, which can be filled up with herbs as necessary.**

Utilitarian style

This loft is home to a couple who have resisted the pull of retirement in the country in favour of a bold reappraisal of city living. Storage is both sensible and adventurous in a kitchen that takes up one corner of one level, where metal-rimmed windows allow light to bounce off glass splashbacks and gleaming stainless-steel accessories.

Chrome, used with discretion, is always capable of pulling a room in a contemporary direction without becoming clichéd. Here it slips neatly onto several surfaces for a unifying visual coherence. Teamed with white cabinets, tall food and larder cupboards and a polished wooden floor, the end result is a sleek mix of functional materials and no-nonsense accessories. Designing cupboards in such a way means they are at home in any room space, whether in the kitchen, living room, bedroom or bathroom, and they make a quiet backdrop to the serious elements of cooking, entertaining and living.

Left **Heaven is a big blue fridge with a plinth all of its own to emphasize the fine contours and bold colour.**

Right **Chunky recessed handles and oversized chrome pull handles emphasize the practicality of this loft kitchen.**

Opposite **A pull-out larder is many people's idea of condiment contentment. Everything is at once visible and accessible: ideal for throwing together an evening snack.**

This page **Find battered kitchenalia in specialist antique stores or garage sales and use them to store unexpected items.**

Right above **Traditional bottle racks are constantly being reinterpreted in new materials, such as bright plastics, chrome and steel.**

Right below **Transparent containers do away with labels, which eventually peel off or wear away.**

Opposite left **If space permits, bread bins are a great asset and can look good on the worktop.**

Opposite right above **A neat chrome trolley will store, transport and display food, china or table linen.**

Opposite right below **Funky metal canisters in a range of sizes make ideal containers for tea, coffee and sugar.**

On the shelf

f you are not someone who likes to keep everything tidied away, feel free to go with your instincts and grasp the notion of big-time display. As long as there is space for everything you need in the kitchen, it doesn't matter that china, utensils and pans mingle together and jostle for space in bazaar-like decoration.

In this converted school house, wicker picnic baskets hide a collection of uninspiring plastic containers and distinctly unstylish colanders and sieves, yet despite the relaxed, casual style, they look neat and controlled lined up in threes in a space beneath the worktop. On the other side of the room, a painted carved French armoire is used as the kitchen larder, and is kept permanently stocked up with tins of vegetables, powdered milk and sauces for impromptu meals.

In a room where storage is so much a part of the decorative order, the addition of an extra-long table and informal chairs creates such a relaxed atmosphere that the absence of conventional solutions, such as built-in units, concealed cupboards and individual cooking, eating and entertaining zones, matters not a bit.

Left **Using an armoire or utility cupboard as a larder is what everyone did before fitted kitchens were invented. The deep shelves in antique cupboards make good minders for key ingredients, such as bulky packets of pasta, oils, mustards and vinegars.**

Right **Keeping all the kitchen equipment out on display means you can always locate what you need and never have to make more than a couple of steps to the nearest pot, pan or utensil.**

Left Larders can be as relaxed in appearance as old cupboards or as sophisticated as pull-out units fitted with individual storage baskets. As long as they are stocked up with good things and you know where to find everything you need, that's all that matters.

Right Supporting a tiled worktop with wooden supports and shelves is an economic alternative to fitting out an entire room. Dot baskets within for keeping larger items out of sight, or else pile up plates, bowls or vases to combine storage with display.

61

Left above **Tucking a small fridge under a worktop is a good way of preserving space. You can always have a large fridge–freezer elsewhere to top up supplies.**

Left below **Chopping boards stack neatly under a table, to be swiftly pulled out when the need takes you.**

This page **An oven, cutlery drawers and appliance cupboards are all neatly housed in a stone cube in front of a supporting pillar where ample sockets allow for a display of useful but beautiful equipment.**

Opposite left above **Washing machines are always more silent tucked behind doors.**

Opposite left below **Food processors save time and energy, but make sure you keep all the attachments safely in one place to preserve your sanity.**

Opposite far right **A big expanse of stainless steel is relieved visually only by a fluorescent kettle on an otherwise empty surface.**

Planning a kitchen around the existing architectural features of the room and incorporating contemporary units without compromising the space has been achieved here with success. One end of the room is devoted to functional, minimalist built-in cupboards that sit well beneath a cool marble worktop. A row of pigeon-holes above the cupboards breaks up the solid expanse of white and provides a good display area for a collection of Grecian-style vases.

At the other end of the room a more relaxed feel is created by the addition of a large wooden dining table, which incorporates a drawer for table linen, and other freestanding wooden units, which add warmth and act as a foil to the modern designs elsewhere. A hefty butcher's block slots neatly into a redundant fireplace where it makes an attractive feature that is useful for display. Fitted with castors, it can easily be pulled out for use as a food preparation area, close to the dining table and adjacent to the well-stocked larder where most of the essential ingredients live. A battered wooden dresser where the china is displayed stands against the opposite

A place for everything

wall. Instead of being used purely for display, this dresser is employed as it was originally intended to be. The white china looks great when it is not in use, and is close to the table when meal times come around. Using a dresser in this way allows precious cupboard space to be devoted to other kitchen equipment that would look less attractive on display.

Opposite **The everyday china on the shelves of a dresser makes a simple display between meal times.**

Right above A generous larder cupboard is kept well stocked with ingredients for impromptu meals.

This page **Unfussy white fitted cupboards provide a home for everything from china to coats.**

Right below Drawers inset below a dining table house table linen and cutlery right where they are needed.

Above **The pink of the units is cleverly offset by the cool, natural shades of the walls, work surfaces and floor, creating a clean, balanced, well-organized space, which is as functional as it is stylish.**

Left **A line of colourful built-in cupboards that match the kitchen units** lead the eye from one end of the house to the other, and embrace all the clutter that no-one wants to see.

Opposite **For an unusual but innovative solution, plates are stored neatly inside deep drawers that have been specially fitted with racks to hold them vertically in an ordered fashion.**

A converted basement is transformed into a stylish, contemporary kitchen that is made light and airy by the brilliant white walls, cool expanses of chrome and wooden worktops, and sand-coloured tiled floor, all of which lend the room a simple, understated feel. In contrast are the bright raspberry-pink units with smart chrome pulls, which provide ample storage for all kitchen equipment, and help to impose order and control in a busy home. The clever combination of colours and materials works well, as the soft, natural tones of the wood, metal and stone prevent the pink from being overpowering.

On the outside, at least, everything is organized, functional and calm. The clutter is contained behind

Cool and sleek with contemporary style

closed doors with only the essential appliances sitting ready in their place of use. Long worktops provide plenty of space for preparing food, and the additional area on the central island, with the row of stools that tuck neatly underneath, is ideal for hasty breakfasts.

Tall cupboards that match the units are built all along one wall of an adjacent hallway to tie the areas together visually and make light work of putting away toys, coats and anything else that could disturb the symmetry of such a balanced, clean space.

Opposite left

**Simple Cornishware china
and a sink area beneath
disguised with gingham
fabric, prove that a
utilitarian kitchen can be
very appealing.**

Opposite right above

**Gilt china stored on
industrial metal shelving
makes a bold display all of
its own.**

Opposite right below

**A wooden cutlery drawer
is perfection itself, with
everything neatly in place.**

Left above **Mesh containers
allow cutlery to drain.**

Left below **Identical glasses
in rows are both pleasing to
look at and invitingly empty.**

Right above **Matching china
stacked in neat piles always
staves off a sense of panic
when all around is chaos.**

Right below

**An ergonomically designed
cutlery drawer allows
simple access from one
compartment to another.**

I n a period house, the kitchen is designed to fit carefully among existing architectural elements, so as to preserve their character while creating an unobtrusive, compact cooking area. The cooker, like all good ranges, is slipped into the fireplace recess. A clock stands on the mantelpiece above as a hint of the room's former use. Next to the cooker, the worktop juts out slightly and is supported by tubular metal poles with shelves at intervals along their length, forming a fixed stand for pots and pans right where you most need it. It also houses a serious collection of cooking oils, vinegars and flavourings.

Tall cupboards with frosted-glass doors make full use of the high ceiling and provide an enticing but not wholly revealing view of the contents within. The upper shelves are filled with less-frequently-used items and are easily accessed when necessary by a pair of stylish fold-out steps, which double as a stool. Fitted units are divided into drawers and feel less formulaic because the wall cupboards are of a different, but sympathetic, design. All the essentials have been incorporated in a compact, ergonomic configuration in keeping with the existing features.

Compact, converted kitchen

Right **A pair of fold-out steps are useful in all rooms of the home: in kitchens for accessing high shelves and cupboards, in children's rooms for reaching the top of the wardrobe to retrieve lost treasures, and in any room with tall windows they are essential for detaching curtains and blinds.**

Far right **A cooking range, worktop and glass-fronted cupboards slip happily in and among an old chimney breast to form a pleasing contemporary kitchen.**

Left **Wall-mounting a conventional plate rack and suspending other cooking implements from a rail saves a great deal of space.**

Below **A purpose-built pot stand juts out from the range but is close to hand for transferring pot to stove.**

71

Left **Knife storage has to be safe and practical. Fitting slots within a kitchen drawer keeps individual pieces stationary, with the blades protected.**

Below **Wall-mounted knife storage is another good way of keeping them out of reach but ready for use.**

Right above **A spirited collection of colanders and jerry cans is brought to life with a garland of colourful flowers.**

Right below **Stainless-steel utensils in upright containers make shiny additions to the areas of kitchen action.**

Far right **Hanging racks need not be elaborate. Inexpensive copper tubing is as good as shiny chrome poles for suspending equipment on butcher's hooks.**

The home office
_____

is here to stay

work station

A working office is an increasingly common feature of many homes. The number of people who now spend all or part of their working week at home with their technology instead of commuting to the office is high, and rising all the time. Where once a humble study sufficed, consisting of no more than a solid oak desk tucked in a corner or under a window, many of today's new homes are being designed to include flexible spaces and rooms that are capable of incorporating a comprehensive home office.

Working from home can play havoc with your storage. Guest bedrooms, dining rooms, conservatories, landings and under-stairs nooks are the spaces most often appropriated by home workers, only to be labelled too small, dark, public and unprofessional by many lapsed office dwellers. The answer is economy. Economy of scale, belongings, filing and equipment. Pare down the essentials to make your working life efficient and go from there. If your work involves a lot of paperwork that needs filing and has to be constantly accessible, you will need, at the very least, an alcove of shelves and a couple of cupboards to sustain all your storage needs. The natural cycle of work essentials, from note pads to stapler, letterheads to CD-ROMs, is one that involves storing them so you can find them, use them,

and keep them for the next time. A good mantra to employ when storing your work items is, 'Find it, Use it, File it, Keep it'. By having everything you may require contained in the immediate vicinity, your working chores will lessen, the ergonomics will function well and your tasks will be completed quicker, making an early decamp to your other life a distinct possibility. Gauge just what

furniture, technology and materials you need to have close by and you will be halfway to creating a successful working environment.

The simplest home office is often more akin to a traditional study area – somewhere quiet to pay bills, plan holidays, catch up on administration and write letters. Such small-scale activities are easily accommodated in corners or halls, but once you work full-time or part-time from home and you need a desk, computer, fax, task lighting and a book shelf, the demands increase. Self-contained, built-in units with neat pull-out drawers, fold-down worktops and miniature screens and keyboards may be the answer if you are prepared to live a scrupulously compact working life. But unless you are one of those people who enjoy order at all costs, labelling every item in your possession and basking in the knowledge that you can locate anything within a minute, you may find yourself rebelling, and spreading out belongings and reference material on the kitchen table at the thought of such restriction.

If you are working from home all the time, try to devote at least one room of the home to an office area. If you have space, it is worth having a self-contained place, which you can go to in the morning and leave at night. For locations, think original. Depending

Modern, flexible houses increasingly incorporate an ergonomic home-office space to suit a more fluid lifestyle.

Keep your work station separate from your leisure areas, whether it's on a landing, or in an attic or outhouse.

on your type of work, a room away from the house, in a converted garage or outhouse, may be more suitable. Craftspeople and artists, in particular, are often more at home in a studio-like environment, whereas more conventional office-based activities can quite happily be carried out in the home. Creating a platform in a room with high ceilings makes good use of space, as does a pull-down desk under the stairs or in an alcove. Under-used landings can be screened off and dedicated to a technology work station, or a garden shed can be transformed into an office away from the

house. If you are a seasoned tea or coffee drinker, you will need a kettle within reasonable walking distance. Loftrooms are great for peace, but hardly practical if your front door and your kitchen where the biscuits are kept are two floors down.

A dual-purpose room, where a workspace has to double as a guest bedroom or dining room, is possible as long as you demarcate the space and keep storage and furniture to a minimum. Sofa beds make good dividers, as do mobile cabinets and screens. Large armoire-like freestanding units are capable of housing all the technology and can be fitted with a pull-out or pull-down worktop. Make sure all the work can be stored unobtrusively or preferably out of sight at the end of each day so your work doesn't impinge on your leisure.

Good lighting and seating are vital. Sacrifice some space if necessary in order to have a proper work chair. It will keep back problems at bay and add comfort to your working day. Preserve as

much natural light as possible – it will keep you cheerful when work problems overcome you, inspiration deserts you or jobs dry up. Some say it is best not to position a work desk directly in front of a window as the view can be distracting. Others think it a valuable diversion.

A work space is one room where the industrial sits happily with the traditional and function can dictate style. Metal filing cabinets and industrial shelving units on castors won't look out of place against a wooden plan chest or glass-fronted oak cabinet. Decorate the space with an eye on the neutral; wood and metal are good companions, as are white and cream.

Let function dictate style in such an ordered environment, and keep your colour scheme neutral.

Think about small-scale storage, too. Boxes, baskets and mobile plastic or metal trolleys are all excellent solutions for paperwork, creative equipment or a compact fax machine.

A vase of favourite flowers and other personal treats are called for in an environment that lacks the constant social contact of a office. When you have to rely on your own company you need good diversions. Lunch-time breaks can be provided by music, the radio, an exercise bike or the telephone for a few calls to friends. You need some distractions from the normal routine and breaks from solitude when you work at home.

orking away from the office is a burgeoning activity, so new homes are being designed with office space in mind and equipped with extra telephone points, sockets for computers and natural light sources. Good storage is important. Depending on your work, you may need reference material and equipment, and a space for meeting clients. You will certainly find that a compact computer, comfortable chair and desk, uncluttered worktop and plenty of shelves are vital if you need to house everything within a limited space. Make use of the entire floor-to-ceiling area to maximize your use of space. Shelves of varying heights will accommodate everything from magazines and files to oversized books and paperbacks, while small drawers, freestanding or incorporated in a larger system, hold stationery.

Include a radio or hi-fi if you are the kind of person who can only work with background noise. A small sink and kettle in a corner will be useful if your kitchen is far away, especially when you are visited by a client. Most importantly, make sure your chair and desk fit your requirements for comfort and ease of work.

Orderly

Left A window allows you a connection with the outside while you bash away at the computer. Have all you need close by and a chair on castors to save time.

Below A cup of tea or glass of wine at the end of a busy day will set you up for the evening.

Right Adjustable shelving makes space for books of all sizes. Fill the top shelves with seldom-used books and keep a ladder handy.

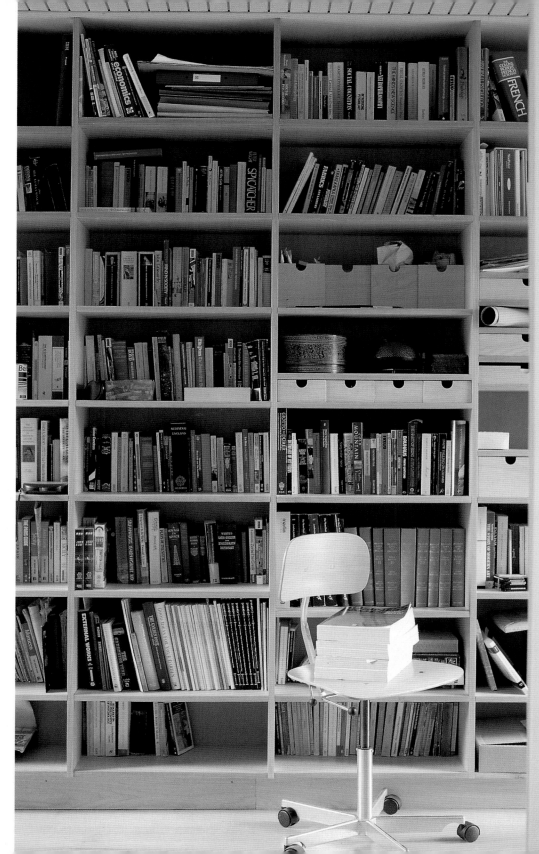

Office in a corner

This page Loose baskets on open
shelving hide paperwork, an old
sewing table makes an informal
desk and a restored plan chest
provides storage space.

Opposite above A whole wall is
devoted to work and is fitted
with shelves and a sideboard
with drawers.

Opposite below left Ample natural
light is cast over this desk, with
a piano behind for diversion.

Opposite below centre All the
shallow drawers in this chest are
catalogued for easy reference.

Opposite below right Fold-up chairs
save space and are easy to store.

Not all home offices have to be neat, structured affairs. Any corner can be given over to a small work space, thinking zone or creative spot. One focal piece of freestanding furniture will set the tone, whether a plan chest, a deep chest of drawers or a simple table – you don't need much to get started. As long as there is enough storage for keeping paperwork under control, you can pay bills, write novels, rebuild a home or start a business from a dresser or kitchen breakfast bar.

Walls are often the best spot for making space. Shallow shelves for keeping books or clutter; pigeon-holes for sorting fabrics, craft materials or stationery; metal shelves for storing CDs and plants – all add something. If space is really tight, try a fold-up table

under a wall-mounted cupboard, or fit out a cupboard with a fold-down desk for an instant office. On an otherwise decorative piece of furniture, place a large wooden box to hold all your work paraphernalia. Use unexpected containers for unappealing junk. Baskets, metal trolleys, battered chests and mobile filing cabinets all store and make a style statement.

Minimal office, maximum storage

Working at home involves clearing the mind of all things domestic, removing yourself from the humdrum of everyday life and escaping to a space where the brain can function creatively and efficiently. Storage plays a strong role in creating the right kind of atmosphere in which to work successfully.

This minimal approach serves several functions. A simple desk with only the necessary elements to hand – computer, stationery, phone and fax, pencils and note pads – is hardworking yet not overwhelming. A light-box for viewing work and large storage boxes for paperwork and other untidy clutter are arranged on movable, adjustable industrial shelving units that are infinitely flexible and don't fill the space. There are no visual distractions to disturb the concentration in this minimal area, and there is still room for the office to expand if need be.

Landings are good places for setting up small offices once sockets and phone lines are installed. Under-stairs cupboards can be taken out to create extra space and mobile storage units moved from room to room if needed. If you have a laptop or computer that lives on a mobile trolley, buy a desk which, when not in use, folds up into a small, stackable square to conserve space. Stacking boxes and files can be placed in mobile units and slotted into cupboards.

Right **Sorted, stacked and thoroughly cool, an office with a simple mission – efficiency.**

Left **Perspex™ folding chairs stack away at night and are unobtrusive additions to a minimal desk.**

Creative space

Left **Prevent the frustrated cry, 'Has anyone see the scissors?' by attaching them to the work surface.**

Right **Numbered pigeon holes are reminiscent of school lockers but seriously sensible for keeping bits and bobs in order.**

Opposite above left
A pinboard, divided into sections with thick tape, makes a graphic framework for photographs and travel memorabilia.

Opposite above right
A galvanized pot attached to the wall makes a great holder for paintbrushes with the added advantage that it cannot be knocked over.

Below **Pens and pencils are contained by a utilitarian metal pot resting, in quirky fashion, on a table mat.**

Whenever creative space is needed, there are usually disparate elements to draw together and keep safe but accessible. Use surprising containers to store everyday items and vice versa. Recycled cans look good en masse filled with pens or brushes; glass jars filled with buttons, braids and shells present their own display; and fabric swatches glued onto shoe boxes for easy identification are a good solution in a sewing room.

Whether a workroom is used for hobbies, to house the sewing machine and artwork, or as a home to a creative profession, like graphic design or costume-making, storing and displaying sources of inspiration becomes a strong part of the story. Displays of personal treasures may appear merely decorative, but will often spark off ideas. Leave space for inspirational items, and for cupboards and plan chests in which to keep completed work in good condition.

Working on
a platform

Converted spaces often have tall, tall ceilings that need exploiting. This platform office lies halfway up the room, with a view onto the living space below. It would all be too distracting were it not for the metal-panelled enclosure, which brings containment and helps to block out noise from elsewhere in the home.

With careful thought and planning, compact offices can be more ergonomically sound than those in large spaces where everything is placed at random in a room. Organized living is the only option in such a small space as this, where a work station stands next to a couple of mobile filing cabinets. That's all there is room for, but all that's required.

Cutting a worktop and shaping it to fit around the contours of a space, or else cutting it away to fit across the corner of a room is a good way of making a difficult space work well for you.

Opposite **Computer, phone, fax and filing are all within easy reach of the desk in this compact space.**

Centre right **Metal shelving reflects and extends the work ethic in an industrial setting.**

Above right **Placing a waste bin next to the printer is always a good move – recycling on a plate.**

Below right **Small cardboard drawers are perfect for keeping stationery in order.**

Sweet dreams for

organized people

comfort zone

The bedroom is the one room in the home that is often dismissed as a place for sleeping and little else, yet it is the space where we spend a third of our lives. A sense of order and aesthetics here is central to a quest for wellbeing. Sensitive architects, exponents of Feng Shui and devotees of natural decorating are united in their belief that bedrooms containing natural materials, built-in storage, good lighting and a sense of space are what we should be striving for, to create somewhere restful, restrained and reviving.

All sorts of disparate belongings find their way into the bedroom. Often it becomes a dumping ground for objects that can't be found space elsewhere, such as musical instruments, album collections, exercise equipment or any books that overspill from the shelves in other rooms. In addition to this incidental clutter is the necessary task of providing space for clothes, shoes, accessories, toiletries and bed linen.

The bed itself should be chosen and positioned with storage as well as a sense of style in mind. As the dominant feature in the room, it is what dictates the look and ethos of the space. Where tall ceilings prevail, a platform bed with a storage or work space beneath provides several solutions in one go. Beds can be as simple as slatted wooden units fitted into a recess with

Of all the rooms in a home, a bedroom should be an oasis of calm – a place where relaxation and rest come easily.

storage above and below, or as ornate as a wrought iron, antique extravaganza with calico drawers on castors underneath for hiding a shoe collection. Nowadays, under-bed storage is far more versatile and sophisticated than the old-fashioned notion of hoarding bank notes under the mattress. Purpose-made drawers, slimline baskets and plastic boxes with lids and castors all provide space for blankets, sports equipment and other items.

Once the bed is chosen and installed, you can exploit the area at the end of the bed. Blanket boxes, trunks, wooden shoe racks and cubes on castors make good storage and display areas. Lying in bed contemplating a vase of favourite flowers, a sculpture or a pile of treasured books at the foot is far more enriching for the soul than gazing at a pile of discarded clothes, old toast and yesterday's newspaper. Using the wall space immediately around the bed will often give further solutions. Building a simple unit on each side and above the head of the bed or sinking the bed itself into an alcove fitted with shelves are economic ways of using space, while having a bed base that sprouts bedside tables on either side as an organic extension to the bed frame is another. Think calm not chaos.

Much can be learned from the storage legacy of the Shakers, a religious movement of the 18th century based on the east coast of the USA. Their approach to life was simple, and every item in their possession was carefully stored in a place of its own, behind doors lovingly fashioned from wood, each joint, hinge and spatial proportion carefully considered and executed. Their designs have become so sought after and influential because they make so much sense in

The bed is the focal point of the room, and whatever the style, it will present all kinds of versatile storage options.

a world where consuming is an obsession, possessions increase to the point of wastefulness and the yearning for a simpler life is an inevitable ambition. The Shakers were among the first designers to resort to built-in cupboards for storing everything from honey to tools, clothing and bed linen.

Tackling the storage of clothes is one of the main priorities in a bedroom. Start with the usual ruthless edit, create the piles to recycle or bin, and think about how you are going to store what's left. Built-in cupboards are the best solution if you are planning to stay

somewhere for a long time. They conserve floor space and allow a good system of organization within. Grade all your clothes by size, then work out how much hanging space you need and at what intervals. Approach the insides of the cupboards as you would those in a kitchen – consider everything you need to store, then buy or build appropriate elements. In the same way that carousel shelves, integral spice racks and pot stands solve specific problems in the kitchen, wardrobes can be kitted out with tie racks and drawers for scarves, socks, jewellery and handkerchiefs, while shoes can be ordered in hanging racks or neatly lined up in pull-out drawers. Don't forget that clothes collections grow as well as shrink, so always allow room for expansion. Plan to install as many rails and shelves as you think you'll need, then add some. Allow space for awkward items, such as hat boxes, and tall slots for sports equipment. Look at shop fittings for ideas and incorporate cardboard

shoes boxes, interior lights, plastic baskets, open shelves and metal rails and boxes on castors as appropriate.

Calculate your hanging needs by allowing a space 60 cm (24 in) wide for coats and dresses and 100 cm (39 in) wide for jackets and shirts. But if all this measuring and calculation is one step too far along the road of self-organization, unfitted furniture could be a more appealing and flexible alternative. Folding or rolling T-shirts and tops is effective for keeping them crease-free; store them in zip-up bags, boxes or plastic cubes to keep the dust out. For a nomadic approach, pile jumpers and trousers into individual dump bins on castors and line them up under a freestanding clothes rail in an alcove. Conceal the area with a calico curtain and enjoy the fact that you can be organized without resorting to total precision.

With freestanding rails and purpose-made racks and drawers, clothes storage has never been so exciting.

Old pieces of furniture, such as armoires, linen cupboards, chests of drawers and dressers can be adapted to hold clothes, shoes, boxes and drawers, while open storage or a combination is visually appealing and versatile. Making the choice between unfitted furniture and built-in cupboards is often easier when faced with a room of irregular proportions, one that is small, or one that has to function as a dual-purpose space, where specific storage ideas will present themselves.

Above **The inside of this ordered wardrobe is compartmentalized, with just the right amount of hanging space for jackets and trousers, shelves for laundered shirts, a deep drawer for sweaters and a shelf for cufflinks and belts, all concealed behind pristine white doors.**

Right **Many people's idea of heaven is a large walk-in wardrobe or dressing room with seemingly endless** space for storing clothes. Reminiscent of shop fittings, this dressing area is fitted with rails for hanging dresses, skirts, shirts and jackets, open pigeonhole shelves for jumpers and tops, which show exactly what's there, with an orderly rack at one end devoted to shoes.

Opposite **It is essential to have plenty of good light in which to examine clothes before wearing them.**

Sorted, stacked and hung

Clothes are never in one place for long. The journey from wearer to wardrobe or wash and back again can be made easier by dedicating a specific space to the sorting and storage of clothes. It makes the ritual of choosing something to wear, checking it for marks and creases, wearing it, then washing and rehanging it an efficient process. A dressing area can be accommodated in a small space at one end of a room or hidden the other side of a false wall, behind a bedhead. Fitting it with pigeonholes for stacking tops, a variety of hanging rails at different heights for jackets, suits and dresses, together with pull-out drawers for accessories and underwear means everything has its place. You can even go one step further and colour code outfits.

93

This page **Scaffolding tubes** surrounding a bed give a certain sense of enclosure, and tie-on calico curtains would provide privacy – the rails can even double up as hanging space for clothes. In this minimal room, a ladder for reaching high storage spaces is used the rest of the time as a temporary book shelf, becoming a work of art in its own right.

Right top **Keep reading matter, photographs and personal possessions in stacking boxes, so they are easily portable and calming to the eye.**

Right below **In a relaxed, informal space, storing a few aesthetically pleasing items, such as glossy books and soft blankets, becomes part of the decorative scheme.**

Freestanding and minimal

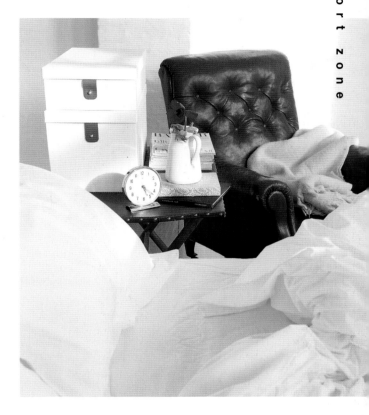

Beds slotted into frames such as scaffolding tubes, wooden four posters, salvaged hospital beds and Shaker bedposts all exploit the potential for additional storage while making a graphic reference point in a bedroom. Add castors to the legs of the frame so you can move the bed around the room when the mood takes you. The antithesis of a built-in bed surrounded with fitted units and shelves, movable beds and furniture allow maximum flexibility and can help to accentuate a sense of space and light, especially in a modern room.

Storage in the form of under-bed boxes, bags and metal trunks are as decorative as they are useful. Make sure any containers can be properly sealed so the contents don't become dusty. Store out-of-season shoes and seldom-worn clothes, bed linen, blankets and sports equipment here, but avoid throwing reams of loose junk into the space; it will quickly gather dust and, knowing it's there, you will put off

looking under the bed indefinitely. A couple of large, movable containers, though, are easy on the eye and are much more manageable to drag clear for cleaning under the bed.

Bedside tables, too, can be movable, foldable and multipurpose. A fold-up table can easily be carried to another room when needed, or indulge yourself at the weekend and use it for eating breakfast. Small wooden, Perspex™ or plastic units on castors are all good alternative solutions for versatile bedside tables.

Left **Sometimes a plain, deep cupboard is all you need for an entire wardrobe, and this elegant piece can move house with its owner.**

Right **Thick, safe-like doors swing open to reveal a carefully thought-out storage plan.**

Below **Swivel drawers conserve space and allow several to be opened at once if a search is on.**

Bottom **Shoes slot comfortably into the remaining spaces.**

The art of clever concealment

Once you have sifted through your wardrobe and discarded anything which is past its style date, worn or faded, it may be worthwhile creating a one-off piece of furniture tailored to your needs. This ordered, elegant wardrobe opens to reveal a tardis-like storage system based on simple clothes retrieval. Interior lighting illuminates suits, jackets and trousers, glass-fronted drawers glide open to reveal colour-coded shirts, ties are hung in a way that displays their pattern. Deep drawers hold sweaters, swivel-mounted boxes fixed into the doors hold cufflinks, spectacles and wallets. A generous mirror allows a final check on the inevitable elegance that follows effortlessly from such organization.

96

Above and below
**See-through containers
are ideal for items of
jewellery, hair accessories
or cotton wool.**

Right above **Pressed shirts
are kept neat stored flat in
individual drawers.**

Right below **The key to an
organized wardrobe is to
group like items and
allocate them a space that
is exclusively their own.**

Top left **Pairs of shoes will remain together and in good condition on special racks.**

Top centre **Drawer organizers will keep socks and tights under control.**

Above **A miniature chest of drawers is perfect for keeping jewellery in order.**

Far left **Tiny compartments store make-up so you can see exactly what's there.**

Left **Narrow shelves with a flat fascia rim will enable you to display rolled-up belts, braces and scarves.**

This page **A versatile wall of storage is pure bliss. How could you not be organized with such a variety of drawers, rails and shelves in such a glorious colour?**

Opposite **A chic floor-to-ceiling storage system incorporates hanging space, lots of cupboards and shoe storage slotted on the end. Neat drawer pulls punctuate the system in regular lines.**

Purpose-built solutions

Above **Generous baskets** slot neatly under a metal bed to hide clutter and form a decorative, ordered line.

Left **Linen baskets** nestle modestly behind a lace curtain for a rural twist.

Opposite top left **Boxes on** top of cupboards provide additional storage space.

Opposite top right **Fill up** a battered old trunk with keepsakes, towels, bed linen or blankets and place it at the end of the bed.

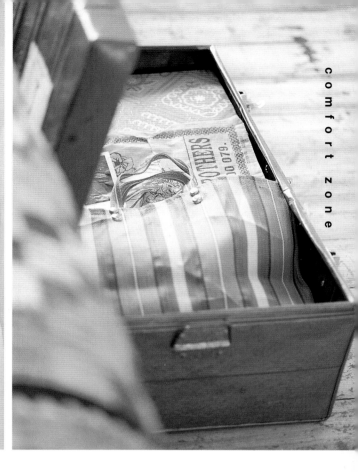

Left **A chest of drawers designed in the style of shop fittings is the perfect see-all clothes storage.**

Out of sight, out of mind

f a strictly regimented built-in policy is simply not you, experiment with freestanding containers and furniture. As long as you have enough space to contain every last piece of clutter, a natural order will emerge. Freestanding pieces can be anything from blanket boxes and tin trunks to cane-panelled cupboards and shop furniture. Any piece of furniture with shelves, compartments, drawers or big doors is at once useful and decorative.

Baskets under beds are good for hair dryers and other ugly but frequently used items. Use them on shelves for bed linen, clean and dirty laundry or children's toys. Retaining an element of visibility will help you identify the contents or at least jog your memory as to the last items you piled in.

Calmness, symmetry and balance prevail in this beacon of modern ethnic design. Every surface, texture and material has been carefully chosen and the furniture crafted in a spirit of creative control. The clever use of colour ensures that the subtle, earthy shades merge unobtrusively from one to another. The walls incorporate flush-fitted cupboards of such finesse that they are enveloped by the space in a fusion of subdued colours. The bedside tables are useful, elegant cubes – even the wardrobe door handles echo the rectangular shapes found everywhere.

Balanced space

Left **Designing storage that merges rather than emerges is a modernist's dream.**

This page **A modest dressing area, where clothes and an easy chair don't hide the view, is neatly tucked behind a knocked-through wall.**

Storing the inevitable toys, clothes and other objects that children gather in great, unwelcome quantities is always a challenge. Many parents see it either as an impossible task, or else they set off on a quest to impose order on everything from books to a mishmash of construction toys, board games and incomplete jigsaw puzzles. Compartmentalized cupboards, boxes, drawers and desks work well when children tidy up after themselves, take pride in their own space and learn to love order. But you may never have time to devise the ultimate dolls' wardrobe system or invent a way of scooping up the teddies' hospital in one easy trawl. Take a deep breath, build lots of cupboards and try the following.

Bunk beds and platform beds can often be built or adapted to include book shelves, work desks, lighting and under-bed drawers. Equally, the dead space under a single bed can be used effectively by filling it with baskets of toys or clothes drawers. Peg rails or wall-mounted canisters can be used to hold puppets, hair bands, drawstring bags of ballet gear, football kit and other items that are needed regularly. Boxes on castors are great for the end-of-the-day swoop to mop up board games, dressing-up clothes and other toys. Hanging clothes rails that can be wheeled about are useful for dressing-up clothes, school uniform and party outfits, while miniature hammocks are a good way of piling up the soft toys.

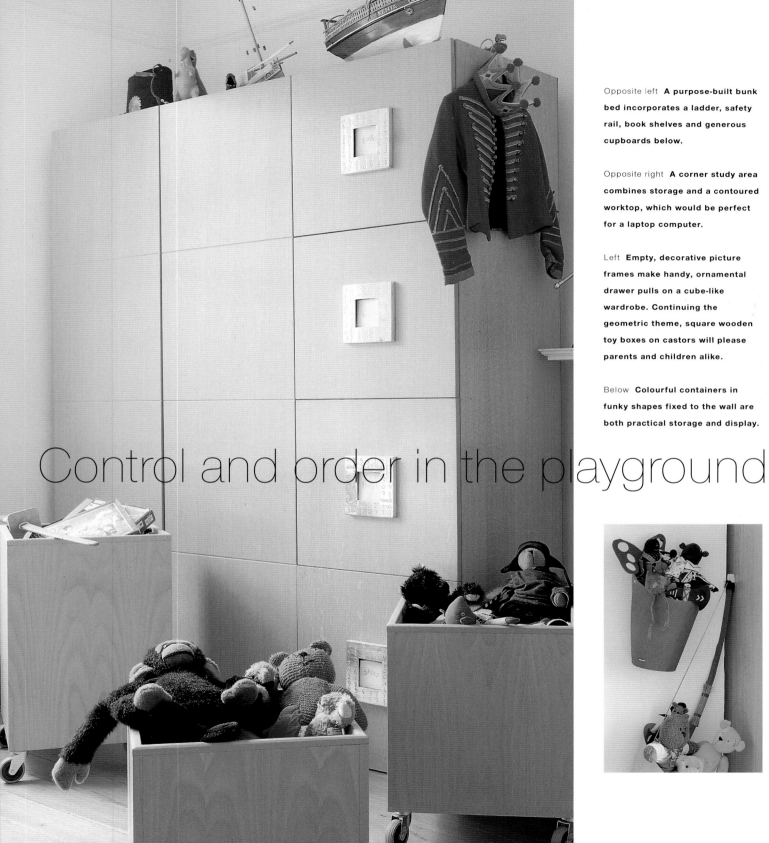

Opposite left **A purpose-built bunk bed incorporates a ladder, safety rail, book shelves and generous cupboards below.**

Opposite right **A corner study area combines storage and a contoured worktop, which would be perfect for a laptop computer.**

Left **Empty, decorative picture frames make handy, ornamental drawer pulls on a cube-like wardrobe. Continuing the geometric theme, square wooden toy boxes on castors will please parents and children alike.**

Below **Colourful containers in funky shapes fixed to the wall are both practical storage and display.**

Control and order in the playground

Clean, calm, revitalized

and ready to go

splash zone

Pure, clean and simple, the bathroom is the place for pale colours, soft textures and natural materials. Try to avoid, or at least minimize, bathroom clutter as much as possible, to create a tranquil setting that promotes a sense of calm for a total spiritual revival.

Once the sanitary fittings are fixed in place, bathroom storage is simply a matter of using any space that is left over in a way that both complements the style of room and ensures maximum efficiency for the grooming process, with optimum enjoyment when it comes to bathing. Much bathroom paraphernalia can be less than wonderful to look at, so some form of concealment is usually necessary, whether in the form of neat built-in cupboards, less structured freestanding units, or informal, natural-coloured calico curtains. Solid materials, such as pastel or frosted glass, sleek beech wood and clean, bright white tiles lend purity to cupboard doors, bath surrounds and splashbacks. Serenity beckons.

Many bathrooms have limited space, so cramming in piles of bath towels and bed linen, reams of toiletries, medicine and first-aid supplies and a laundry basket are often challenging storage exercises. As with kitchens, the smaller the space the more likely you are to benefit from some kind of built-in unit. Maybe one under the sink for storing all the cleaning materials or

a bath built into a recess that has shelves above and cupboards at either side. Safe storage is especially important in the bathroom, particularly for sharp implements, toxic cleaning materials and pills and medicines, which should always be kept in a lockable cabinet and out of the reach of children. Wall-mounted cabinets, either fitted with or without mirrors, are ideal for storing medicines. Many toiletries are packaged in visually pleasing bottles and jars that make a good display if they are left out when not in use. Narrow tongue-and-groove open shelves along one or more walls are the perfect way to store and display such items so that you can always see exactly what's there.

In a small bathroom, you will feel instantly better about the lack of space if the towels are of good quality and a pleasing colour; shampoo, bubble bath and shower gel bottles look appealing rather than being plastered with a frenzy of advertising and labels, and soap; shaving equipment, toothpaste and cotton wool are kept in attractive, interesting containers. Choose good-looking bars of soap and display them well in metal or wicker baskets, glass dishes or metal trays.

When there is room in the bathroom for an easy chair, choose one with a lift-up seat that doubles as a laundry basket or a place to store clean towels, or clip a shelf onto the chair back for storing toys, body brushes or toilet rolls. In a small room, a folding chair or a stool that tucks underneath the sink or behind the door will conserve space. If the bathroom is large enough, incorporate a row of low-level cupboards along one wall for paraphernalia and place bench cushions along the top. Fix a shelf close to the WC for some

The bathroom should be more than a place to wash, it should be an oasis of calm where the spirits are revived.

Pare down the clutter and make sure you have room to keep luxurious treats to pamper yourself after a long day.

books, magazines and newspapers. Glass shelves are always pleasing in a bathroom, since the light that bounces off mirrors, taps and gleaming sinks is reflected and enhanced as it hits glass surfaces.

Alternatively, dispense with shelves and install a large, long peg rail instead. Two pegs for each member of the family – one for towels and one for a drawstring bag of dirty laundry or personal toiletries. Use the back of the door for coat hooks so gowns and robes can keep dry. Store towels either on traditional freestanding towel rails, on wall-mounted and heated chrome rails or on pivoting rails fixed to the wall. Make sure they are within easy reach of the sink, shower or bath to be ergonomically sound. Freestanding furniture such as linen cupboards or movable cupboards and trolleys are also good ways of storing spare towels, clean bed linen and extra blankets on secondment from the bedroom.

In showers, a neat wall-hung metal shower tidy will contain all the shampoos, conditioners and soaps you are likely to need. Clip additional plastic hanging rails over a shower door to hold a towel, slippers and spectacles. Bath racks placed over the bath are a good way of keeping everything you need for a relaxing soak to hand.

Supplement with a book holder, a glass of wine and a scented candle for relaxing night-time indulgence.

The bathroom is often a good place for a dressing table and full-length mirror (as long as you don't mind the scales having the same home). Sometimes it makes sense for bathrooms to be sited near a utility room. It is not difficult to adapt a bathroom annexe to include

a washing machine and tumble drier, in which case the natural life cycle of dirty clothes leaving a person, going into the laundry basket and thence to the washing machine is considerably speeded up. Add a ceiling-mounted hanging rack over the bath for clothes to dry on, and a couple of hours of spare time beckon. This also ensures that all laundry is neatly contained in one area rather than allowing it to spread over several rooms. In small utility areas washing machines can be stacked on top of dryers to conserve space and hidden behind cupboard doors, which may also incorporate a fold-down ironing board and other cleaning materials, as well as laundry baskets for colour coding the wash or to accommodate the clean, dry 'to iron' pile. Fit laundry baskets with lift-out baskets to make transporting dirty clothes to the washing machine quicker and easier. Then return the inner basket to the utility area full of clothes

Make a display of pleasing bottles and soaps, and use soft, natural-fibre towels in soothing colours.

that are ready to iron. Alternatively, use a stylish, modern fabric laundry bag fixed onto a metal or wooden frame on castors for wheeling easily from room to room to collect the dirty clothes.

The bathroom is an obvious place for displaying a collection of water-related treasures. Fossils, model boats and pretty shells make wonderful seaside still lifes on shelves or other surfaces, while worn glass fragments and stones piled into glass tanks evoke a sense of the coast and allow us a moment's mental transportation. Protect any delicate wooden surfaces with a few layers of matt varnish to prevent condensation or splashes causing damage.

Left **The open shelf under the built-in sink unit breaks up the expanse of wood and prevents it from dominating.**

Right **Coloured and natural baskets in sisal and wicker scoop up all the usual bath-room paraphernalia and provide decoration with their repeating patterns.**

Opposite **Ultra-sleek wall-mounted taps and a stylish glass sink, which rests unobtrusively on a built in unit, conserve space for all-important grooming.**

The art of control and display

The art of control is nowhere better exemplified than in this bathroom, where everything is neatly stored but still visible and accessible. Such a keen sense of order instills purpose and energy at the beginning of the day and a pervading aura of calm at night. The storage is a combination of built-in and stand-alone units that are all perfectly functional and provide a natural home for everything. The array of baskets house difficult-to-store items in sensible, contained order, including rolled-up pastel towels that are easy to grab hold of, and add colour and texture to the otherwise-neutral decor. A recess between the door and unusual built-in sink unit is put to good use with floor-to-ceiling pigeonhole shelves.

reate visual peace and inner harmony in a neutral bathroom by
choosing easy containers in glass, plastic or delicate porcelain and
scrupulously white bath linens. A room that is clean, white and airy, with
good lighting and a firm control of space promotes peace, and carefully planned
storage helps to maintain the sense of calm. Keep towels, toiletries, accessories
and medicines under control in hidden spaces or on discreet display to allow
the space around you to breathe, soothe and heal.

Bathing is one of life's repeated pleasures, a constant cycle of renewal, which
revives and restores the balance of a busy live. Organizing a bathroom so you can
wash, groom, bathe, shower, dry and preen means that the storage must work for
you as much as the space does. Unsightly cleaning equipment should be kept out
of sight, while toiletries and towels should be easy to reach and appealing.

Pure, clean and simple

Opposite top **Soaps are stored in simple porcelain soap dishes.**

Opposite centre **Unobtrusive containers in different sizes have understated style lined up on a shelf.**

Opposite bottom **A clean bath mat is at the ready draped over the edge of the bathtub.**

This page **A clutter-free bathroom is the epitome of tranquility; for creating a sense of calm and restoring peace of mind, there is nothing better than the combination of natural wood and pure white.**

Top right **Pristine towels are piled up next to the basin, right where they're needed.**

Bottom right **A laundry basket is kept in the hallway, en route from the bathroom to the utility room.**

This bold homage to high tech incorporates a grooming area, clothes store and bathroom in a large, light-filled space. Strictly industrial materials, such as rubber flooring, a modernist pedestal sink unit and frosted, sliding panels merge happily with a contemporary take on a 1930s dressing table and two seaside-inspired semicircular canvas screens that offer privacy without obscuring the light. One canvas cubicle encloses a freestanding bath;

Sleek, stylish industrial grooming

another conceals a floor-draining shower. Along one wall, clothes are kept behind the doors, always at hand to slip into once the grooming is complete.

Opposite **A chrome chest of drawers is both toiletries store and reflective surface for the other shiny planes and chrome accessories and fittings elsewhere in the bathroom.**

Left **Flexible storage in the form of hanging rails, shelves and drawers are discreetly stowed behind semi-opaque sliding doors, which also conceal the WC.**

Above **Chrome towel rails are integral to the pedestal sink units and swivel conveniently for use.**

Right **Folding steps allow access to the upper reaches of the wardrobe. The sliding doors can be left open for clothes to be selected from the comfort of the bath.**

Rooms for storage

splash zone

Opposite left **The most humble contents can be given graphic resonance by the right container.**

Opposite top right **Freestanding chrome trays, with handles for easy portability, are ideal for storing wellpackaged toiletries.**

Opposite bottom right **Discarded medical equipment eases the pressure on toothbrush storage.**

Left **A dressing table incorporates storage for grooming equipment, while a miniature plastic chest of drawers holds and displays jewellery and accessories.**

Left below **The bath tidy: simple, useful and strangely elegant over a gleaming white bath, stacked with pleasing bath-time treats.**

Right above **Unexpected containers often double as display. Multicoloured nylon shopping bags house clean towels and transport dirty ones to the laundry basket.**

Right **Soaps in multicultural wrappers are far too gorgeous to store in a cupboard; they need a home where they can be seen.**

Pure Greek olive-oil soap

Kutir

FLOWER BRAND

Opposite **Bathing becomes an ethereal experience in a bathroom divided from the bedroom by double doors, which open to allow light to dance over all the surfaces.**

Left **Natty Perspex™ cubes serve the dual function of protecting fragile fossils and providing a perfect showcase for the collection.**

Right **Towels, clothes and art mingle in a room where display and storage are one and the same.**

Showcase solutions

Sometimes the bathroom is the only logical place for housing a personal collection of water-related treasures. In this big, white space, large windows cast natural light and an aura of calm onto a stunning collection of fragile, translucent fossils placed within a purpose-built arrangement of wooden pigeonholes that make a focal point of the area above the sink. The unit is set against a mirrored alcove and protrudes slightly from the wall to accommodate square Perspex™ cubes, each one housing a different, delicate cargo. The light which comes into the room bounces back and forth between the wall and mirror in a cheering manner. A sandstone surround to the bath and sink provides a textural reference to the collection and, in turn, is home to bowls of large shells and water-smoothed pebbles. Making a virtue and a feature of your collections and belongings in this manner means they are always accessible and available to enjoy and at the same time, make a room uniquely yours.

Bed and table linens, towels and clothes are never static for long. Unlike a jewellery box or tie collection that stay in one place, they follow a changing cycle as they move from dirty linen basket to washer, dryer, ironing basket, then back to a cupboard before the process begins again. Storing such frequently moving items so they progress through all the stages with a minimum of pile-building, sock-losing and ironing overload is almost a scientific task. As is often true, lots of storage can work wonders. Helpful solutions are to have baskets, maybe with castors, in the bedroom, by the washer, and wherever the ironing is done, and plenty of hangers to hand.

Ironing out those creases

This page and opposite

Ironing becomes less of a chore when you use such pleasing equipment as this. A potentially under-used space is put to excellent use with a utilitarian glass-fronted linen cupboard, which encourages tidiness since the contents are always on display. The stairs provide a temporary hanging space and the sturdy, generously proportioned cherry wood ironing board has a fold-out shelf for ironed items. The scaled-down industrial-style laundry bag can be wheeled away and the ironing board tucked beside the cupboard when the work is done.

Source directory

Kitchens

Bulthaup
37 Wigmore Street
London W1H 9LD
Clean, contemporary kitchen furniture.

Chalon
The Plaza 535 King's Road
London SW10 0SZ
Unfitted plain and painted kitchen furniture.

Divertimenti
139–41 Fulham Road
London SW3 6SD
Mail order 0171 386 9911
Cooking equipment, storage containers and china.

IKEA
2 Drury Way
North Circular Road
London NW10 0TH
Kitchen units, furniture and general storage.

David Mellor
4 Sloane Square
London SW1W 8EE
Kitchen equipment and china.

de Mornay Boyes Ltd
Unit 2, Thrales End Farm
Thrales End
Harpenden
Hertfordshire AL5 3NS
Hand-built kitchens to any specification.

Newcastle Furniture Company
79 Moore Park Road
London SW6 2HH
Hand-built kitchens in a variety of styles.

Plain English
The Tannery
Combs
Stowmarket
Suffolk IP14 2EN
Traditional hand-built kitchen furniture.

Poggenpohl Group UK Ltd
Silbury Court
368 Silbury Boulevard
Central Milton Keynes
Buckinghamshire MK9 2AF
High-quality, custom-designed fitted kitchen furniture.

Rhode Design Furniture Ltd
137–39 Essex Road
London N1 2NR
Shaker-style fitted kitchens.

Slingsby
Preston Street
Bradford BD7 1JF
Industrial metal shelving and storage equipment.

Smeg (UK)
Corinthian Court
80 Milton Park
Abingdon
Oxfordshire OX14 4RY
Streamlined stainless-steel kitchen appliances.

Summerill & Bishop
100 Portland Road
London W11 4LN
Rustic French accessories for the kitchen and home.

Furniture and storage units

Aero
96 Westbourne Grove
London W2 5RT
Contemporary furniture and accessories for all around the home.

The Conran Shop
Michelin House
81 Fulham Road
London SW3 6RD
Contemporary accessories.

The CubeStore
38 Grosvenor Road
London W4 4EG
Modular storage systems.

The Futon Company
169 Tottenham Court Road
London W1P 9LH
Futons in all shapes and sizes.

General Trading Company
144 Sloane Street
London SW1X 9BL
Furniture and home accessories.

Grand Illusions
2–4 Crown Road
St Margarets
Twickenham
Middlesex TW1 3EE
French country furniture for workrooms, living rooms, kitchens and bedrooms.

Habitat
196 Tottenham Court Road
London W1P 9LD
Home accessories and furniture.

Heal's

196 Tottenham Court Road

London W1P 9LD

Contemporary furniture and accessories and storage for all around the home.

The Holding Company

243–45 King's Road

London SW3 5EL

Mail order 0171 610 9160

A complete range of innovative storage solutions for every room in the home.

Hülsta Furniture (UK) Ltd

22 Bruton Street

London W1X 7DA

Fitted cabinets for all rooms.

Jerry's Home Store

163–67 Fulham Road

London SW3 6SN

Contemporary and traditional furniture and accessories from the USA.

McCord Mail Order

Universal House

Devonshire Street

Manchester M60 6EL

0990 53 54 55

General home accessories and furniture by mail order.

The Pier

200 Tottenham Court Road

London W1P 9LA

Furniture and storage solutions and lots of general home accessories.

The Shaker Shop

25 Harcourt Street

London W1H 1DT

Shaker-style furniture and accessories.

Sofa Workshop

324–26 King's Road

London SW3 5UH

Sofas in all shapes, styles and colours.

Small-scale storage

Blakes English Willow Shop

3 Chapel Yard

Holt

Norfolk NR25 6HG

Hand-made willow baskets, trugs and garden accessories.

Cubbins & Company

Unit 1, Rampisham Manor

Dorchester

Dorset DT2 0PT

Top-quality decorative boxes, waste bins and linen baskets.

The Holding Company

243–45 King's Road

London SW3 5EL

Mail order 0171 610 9160

Novel storage solutions.

IKEA

2 Drury Way

North Circular Road

London NW10 0TH

Furniture and storage.

Lakeland Plastics Ltd

Alexandra Buildings

Windermere

Cumbria LA23 1BQ

Mail order 015394 88100

Small-scale solutions for all rooms.

Muji

26 Great Marlborough Street

London W1V 1HL

Understated Japanese solutions.

Humphrey Newcome Marketing

7c Church Street

Dronfield

Sheffield S18 1QB

Coloured plastic boxes in all sizes.

Paperchase

213 Tottenham Court Road

London W1P 9AF

Contemporary and fun small-scale.

Purves & Purves

80–1 & 83 Tottenham Court Road

London W1P 9HD

Contemporary British and European design.

The Source

26–40 Kensington High Street

London W8 4PF

Furniture, units and lots of small-scale storage solutions for every room in the home.

Workspaces

Bisley Office Furniture

FC Brown (Steel Equipment) Ltd

Queens Road

Bisley

Surrey GU24 9BJ

Industrial metal filing cabinets.

Office World

339 The Hyde

Edgware Road

London NW9 6TH

Everything for the home office.

Ryman the Stationer

Ryman House

Swallowfield Way

Hayes

Middlesex UB3 1DQ

Stationery and storage.

Acknowledgements

1 a house in London designed by Guy Stansfeld 0171-727 0133; 2 Dawna & Jerry Walter's house in London; 3 left Paula Pryke's house in London; 3 right Vanessa & Robert Fairer's studio in London designed by Woolf Architects 0171-428 9500; 4 centre the London flat of Miles Johnson & Frank Ronan; 4 right Vanessa & Robert Fairer's studio in London designed by Woolf Architects 0171-428 9500; 5 Rosa Dean & Ed Baden-Powell's apartment in London, designed by Urban Salon 0171-357 8800; 6 above Vanessa & Robert Fairer's studio in London designed by Woolf Architects 0171-428 9500; 6–7 Rosa Dean & Ed Baden-Powell's apartment in London, designed by Urban Salon 0171-357 8800; 8–9 Robert Kimsey's apartment in London designed by Gavin Jackson 0705 0097561; 9 the London flat of Miles Johnson & Frank Ronan; 10 left Paula Pryke's house in London; 10 above right Paula Pryke's house in London; 10 centre a house in London designed by François Gilles and

Dominique Lubar, IPL Interiors; 10 below The London flat of Miles Johnson & Frank Ronan; 11 centre left Ian Bartlett & Christine Walsh's house in London; 11 below left Paula Pryke's house in London; 11 right Vanessa & Robert Fairer's studio in London designed by Woolf Architects 0171-428 9500; 12–13 Architecture & furniture by Spencer Fung Architects tel/fax 0181-960 9883; 13 above left Paula Pryke's house in London; 13 centre left Dawna & Jerry Walter's house in London; 13 below left Vanessa & Robert Fairer's studio in London designed by Woolf Architects 0171-428 9500; 14 left a house in London designed by Guy Stansfeld 0171-727 0133; 15 above left a house in London designed by François Gilles and Dominique Lubar, IPL Interiors; 15 right Architecture & furniture by Spencer Fung Architects tel/fax 0181-960 9883; 16–17 David Jermyn's house in London, designed by Woolf Architects 0171-428 9500; 18 Robert Kimsey's apartment in London designed by Gavin Jackson 0705

0097561; 19 left Robert Kimsey's apartment in London designed by Gavin Jackson 0705 0097561; 19 right Vanessa & Robert Fairer's studio in London designed by Woolf Architects 0171-428 9500; 20–23 David Jermyn's house in London, designed by Woolf Architects 0171-428 9500; 23 Robert Kimsey's apartment in London designed by Gavin Jackson 0705 0097561; 24 Rosa Dean & Ed Baden-Powell's apartment in London, designed by Urban Salon 0171-357 8800; 25 Architecture & furniture by Spencer Fung Architects tel/fax 0181-960 9883; 27 left Rosa Dean & Ed Baden-Powell's apartment in London, designed by Urban Salon 0171-357 8800; 28–29 Robert Kimsey's apartment in London designed by Gavin Jackson 0705 0097561; 29 above left Paula Pryke's house in London; 29 below left David Jermyn's house in London, designed by Woolf Architects 0171-428 9500; 29 right Robert Kimsey's apartment in London designed by Gavin Jackson 0705 0097561; 30–31 A house in London designed by Guy Stansfeld 0171-727 0133; 32-33 Paula Pryke's house in London; 34

Vanessa & Robert Fairer's studio in London designed by Woolf Architects 0171-428 9500; 34–35 Dawna & Jerry Walter's house in London; 35 left Vanessa & Robert Fairer's studio in London designed by Woolf Architects 0171-428 9500; 35 right David Jermyn's house in London, designed by Woolf Architects 0171-428 9500; 36–39 Architecture & furniture by Spencer Fung Architects tel/fax 0181-960 9883; 40 left Dawna & Jerry Walter's house in London; 40 centre Rosa Dean & Ed Baden-Powell's apartment in London, designed by Urban Salon 0171-357 8800; 40–43 Rosa Dean & Ed Baden-Powell's apartment in London, designed by Urban Salon 0171-357 8800; 44 left the London flat of Miles Johnson & Frank Ronan; 44 above right Vanessa & Robert Fairer's studio in London designed by Woolf Architects 0171-428 9500; 44 below right Rosa Dean & Ed Baden-Powell's apartment in London, designed by Urban Salon 0171-357 8800; 45 Vanessa & Robert Fairer's studio in London designed by Woolf Architects 0171-428 9500; 46 Dawna & Jerry Walter's house in London; 49 below Dawna & Jerry

Walter's house in London; 52-53 Dawna & Jerry Walter's house in London; 56 below right Dawna & Jerry Walter's house in London; 57 above right Ian Bartlett & Christine Walsh's house in London; 62 above left Vanessa & Robert Fairer's studio in London designed by Woolf Architects 0171-428 9500; 62 right Robert Kimsey's apartment in London designed by Gavin Jackson 0705 0097561; 63 above left Paula Pryke's house in London; 63 right Paula Pryke's house in London; 66–67 a house in London designed by Guy Stansfeld 0171-727 0133; 68 left the London flat of Miles Johnson & Frank Ronan; 68 above right Paula Pryke's house in London; 68 below right the London flat of Miles Johnson & Frank Ronan; 69 above right Dawna & Jerry Walter's house in London; 70–71 Ian Bartlett & Christine Walsh's house in London; 73 above left the London flat of Miles Johnson & Frank Ronan; 73 right Ian Bartlett & Christine Walsh's house in London; 75 a house in London designed by François Gilles and Dominique Lubar, IPL Interiors; 76 above right a house in London designed by François Gilles and

Dominique Lubar, IPL Interiors; 77 left the London flat of Miles Johnson & Frank Ronan; 77 David Jermyn's house in London, designed by Woolf Architects 0171-428 9500; 78–79 Ian Bartlett & Christine Walsh's house in London; 81 above the London flat of Miles Johnson & Frank Ronan; 81 below left a house in London designed by Guy Stansfeld 0171-727 0133; 84 left the London flat of Miles Johnson & Frank Ronan; 84–85 the London flat of Miles Johnson & Frank Ronan; 88 a house in London designed by François Gilles and Dominique Lubar, IPL Interiors; 89 Vanessa & Robert Fairer's studio in London designed by Woolf Architects 0171-428 9500; 90 above left & below Paula Pryke's house in London; 90 above right Dawna & Jerry Walter's house in London; 91 left Paula Pryke's house in London; 91 above right a house in London designed by François Gilles and Dominique Lubar, IPL Interiors; 91 below right a house in London designed by François Gilles and Dominique Lubar, IPL Interiors; 92-93 a house in London designed by François Gilles and Dominique Lubar, IPL Interiors; 94-

95 Vanessa & Robert Fairer's studio in London designed by Woolf Architects 0171-428 9500; 96-97 a house in London designed by François Gilles and Dominique Lubar, IPL Interiors; 98 left Paula Pryke's house in London; 98 right a house in London designed by François Gilles and Dominique Lubar, IPL Interiors; 99 above left a house in London designed by François Gilles and Dominique Lubar, IPL Interiors; 99 above centre, above right & below Paula Pryke's house in London; 100 Ian Bartlett & Christine Walsh's house in London; 101 a house in London designed by Guy Stansfeld 0171-727 0133; 102 above Dawna & Jerry Walter's house in London; 102–103 Architecture & furniture by Spencer Fung Architects tel/fax 0181-960 9883; 103 left Dawna & Jerry Walter's house in London; 103 right the London flat of Miles Johnson & Frank Ronan; 104–105 Architecture & furniture by Spencer Fung Architects tel/fax 0181-960 9883; 106 a house in London designed by Guy Stansfeld 0171-727 0133; 109 Robert Kimsey's apartment in London designed by Gavin Jackson 0705 0097561; 110 above

right Paula Pryke's house in London; 110 below Vanessa & Robert Fairer's studio in London designed by Woolf Architects 0171-428 9500; 111 a house in London designed by François Gilles and Dominique Lubar, IPL Interiors; 112–113 Dawna & Jerry Walter's house in London; 116–117 Paula Pryke's house in London; 118 left & above right Paula Pryke's house in London; 118 below right the London flat of Miles Johnson & Frank Ronan; 119 above left Paula Pryke's house in London; 119 below right the London flat of Miles Johnson & Frank Ronan; 120–121 a house in London designed by Guy Stansfeld 0171-727 0133; 122–123 Vanessa & Robert Fairer's studio in London designed by Woolf Architects 0171-428 9500; 128 Dawna & Jerry Walter's house in London.

The publishers would like to thank the following companies for loaning props for photography for this book:

Grand Illusions, The Holding Company, McCord Storage, Paperchase.

Authors' acknowledgements

We would like to thank the multi-talented Andrew Wood for his
funky photography and good company and the marvellous Melanie Molesworth
for her effortless style. Special thanks to Nadine Bazar and Karina Garrick,
and warm thanks to the wonderful team at RPS: Jacqui Small, Anne Ryland,
Kate Brunt, Zia Mattocks and Ashley Western.

Thanks to our photographic models: Kate Brunt, Becky Davies,
Elizabeth of Mar, Zia Mattocks, Melanie Molesworth, Ashley Western and
Andrew Wood. And thanks to Melanie Molesworth's assistant, Serena Hanbury.

Many thanks also to the people who allowed us to photograph their homes.